PLASTIC SOLDIERS

RANDY ROSNESS

CONTENTS

1

IN THE BEGINNING

I n February of 1947, a small baby boy, Randy, was born in Wichita, Kansas, the very center of the United States at that time. He joined an older sister, Melody, an older brother, Mickey, and eventually a younger sister, Melinda. Randy's biological father was a handsome, athletic, gifted artist, with a beautiful singing voice and just recently admitted into the Army prior to the Korean War. It was shortly after that point that Randy's father, for whatever reason, left his twenty four year old beautiful wife, Betty, and their four children in dire straits. Betty did not have any sort of career at this time. The only way she could keep her four children was to find a home for them. She wouldn't allow them to be adopted by strangers or family members. They were hers! It was shortly after that point that Randy and his older sister, older brother, and baby sister were accepted into the Wichita Children's Home in 1950, at the ages of seven, five, three, and one. Randy and little Melinda were too young to remember their initial delivery and placement. It was probably a much more traumatic memorable experience for Melody and Mickey. Betty, while working two or three jobs at a time, rented a small apartment for herself. The children would join her on weekends when her work schedule permitted. She would notify the Children's Home in advance, and in turn, the Home would prepare the children to leave for the weekend. On rare occasions of military leave, Betty's estranged husband would return for short visits at the apartment. Randy's only childhood remembrance of seeing his father was when he was around three or four years old, and fell out of the top bunk in Betty's apartment. His father came into the bedroom to see what had happened, spanked Randy for the disturbance, and scolded him, saying "I don't want to hear another peep out of you!" At which point, Mickey, from his bottom bunk, softly whispered "peep" as the door closed. It would be over twenty years before Randy would see his father again; and only then because his sister, Melody, was dying of colon cancer in California. There were rare occasions when Betty was unable to break away from her work schedule and could not show up for the children. Patiently waiting in the hallway for their mother, news would come that she would not be able to visit them that evening. The dejection was extremely painful, for both Betty and her kids. Her ex-husband provided no child support during the five years the children were at the Wichita Children's Home. Betty worked two or three part time jobs during those five years to pay the very minimal charges at the home. The children were only allowed to visit their mother one weekend a month and spend two weeks during the year with their grandparents in Oklahoma City, and then return to the Children's Home to their "regular" life.

2

THE NEW NORMAL

Daily life at the Children's Home was really all that Randy knew at his young age. The children who were old enough, would walk to the nearby grade school in groups. If the weather was cool, they would draw gloves, jackets, and hats out of cardboard boxes to wear; a routine that was expedited by the counselors each morning. There was also a small playground area at the Home filled with rocky sand, where the children would meet, weather permitting. Teeter-totters, slides, swings, and monkey bars provided some fun times, as well as much needed exercise. Randy and Melinda would often get together at playtime and sit in the sand. They would pick out some of the larger shiny rock pieces and crack them open to see if they sparkled, and then treat them like jewels. Melody could always be found hovering around when her two youngest siblings were together on the playground. She was a "helicopter sister," long before the term "helicopter" became popular fifty years later.

It was Sunday morning, a fall day in Wichita, Kansas around 1952. City buses were parked outside the old red brick building. About eighty children, the five to twelve year olds, filed out, walked down the front stairs, and took their seats on the buses. As the children climbed aboard their assigned bus to attend church, they were each given a Buffalo Indian Head Nickel to place in the church offering, a tradition that was followed each Sunday. Pulling away from the grounds, the children were able to catch a quick glimpse of the large, ominous, brick and stone boiler building. It emitted steam and odd noises in an effort to heat the main residential quarters, as winter weather was definitely on its way! The multi-acre Children's Home facilities were surrounded by a row of stoic older homes inhabited by senior citizens, mostly elderly widows.

As the bus made the journey toward the downtown Wichita Church of God, the children laughed, played "hand-games," and very often joined in song; "Agga Zigga Zumba... zumba, zumba," "Ten Little Indian Boys," "London Bridge is Falling Down," "The Hokey Pokey;" all the songs of the '50's children.

When they arrived in front of the church, they quietly walked from the bus up the sidewalk, through the beautiful wooden front doors with polished brass hardware, and proceeded upstairs to the secluded loft area where they occupied most of the seating, along with their counselors. Tight supervision, and the fear of potential discipline back at the home, made for a pretty orderly group. The passing of the collection plate was the highlight of the worship service for the children, who felt very much a part of something other than their normal routine by dropping their nickels into the offering plates. Singing hymns was right behind the nickels! When the hour was over, it was time to head back and quickly find the bathroom.

Sunday evening, the huge dining room area was packed

with all of the children around two years and up. The long lines of tables and chairs were completely filled with hungry eyes, mouths, and tummies. Little hands holding forks and spoons. The kitchen/dining staff placed a plate of food in front of each of the children. Now Randy was a very strong-willed five year old; admitted to the home when he was not quite three. As he surveyed his plate, he noticed something very green and weird looking, at least in his mind. It was more commonly known as "spinach." While the other children finished their meals and left the room one at a time, Randy remained in his seat, staring at the strange, untouched, green, slimy substance. Finally, now sitting totally alone, one of the counselors came to him and asked what was wrong. Randy replied, "I can't eat this green stuff." The counselor replied sternly, "Oh yes you will. You will stay here until your plate is clean!" The dining hall lights started shutting down, but Randy remained unmoved; fearfully mesmerized by the green "unknown" third course, and the potential consequences he might suffer for not clearing his plate. The exasperated attendant finally ordered him to his room with a very harsh warning that his attitude would not be tolerated!

The fall days continued; getting colder and colder, shorter and shorter. The spring and summer invasion of the rare cicadas had passed. No more strange, craggy noises to be heard from the scary outer space creatures. Their grizzly shed shells clinging to tree branches no longer remained to remind the children of their strange appearance every few years. Now, a similarly timed human event was taking place - the United States presidential election. "We Like Ike" signs and banners were appearing everywhere. Dwight D. Eisenhower, the brilliant general in World War II and a Kansas "favored son" was now running for President. Many of the children, while clearly aware of the recent end of the war and the return of our military heroes, were totally oblivious to politics. After all, Thanksgiving was on the near horizon, with Christmas, and a brand new year shortly after that. Not to mention school vacations and family visits! They had more pleasant things to consider than a presidential election.

3

INSIDE THE DORM

In the evening time during the week days after dinner, the children would gather in a large meeting room and watch the nightly news on the recently donated black and white 14" TV screen. John Cameron Swayze and Huntley-Brinkley newscasts were chosen by staff members, definitely not the children. Davy Crockett, Gunsmoke, Howdy Doody, and Disney would have to wait outside these walls. But, they all sat on the floor and watched until it was time to go to bed at 8:00 P.M. "Early to bed - early to rise" was a common mantra for the children. Tomorrow would bring chores to be done, breakfast awaiting, and school to attend nine months out of the year. Children, as young as five years old, were expected to fold clothes, make beds, and scrub floors daily. The discipline was rigid, but not "cruel and unusual." It primarily included "reminder" tactics such as a soft board paddling, sitting alone, or having mouths washed out with Epsom salt, for perceived, if not actual, lies. Nothing at all brutal, but memorable lessons in the young children's minds that there were consequences for bad behavior. They were taught to brush their teeth daily, and wash their hands and face before leaving each day and before and after meals. Showers were taken by gender age groups. Randy, having a very modest demeanor, felt uncomfortable with the two or three female attendants watching, talking, and giggling together as the young boys showered. It seemed as if the entire staff at the home was female, except for two or three men who did the equipment maintenance, and who were rarely seen. This was probably a little unsettling for those young boys who either didn't have male role models, or didn't know their fathers.

The occupants of the Home were foster children, orphans, or children temporarily placed by a parent or parents who were unable to care for them during difficult times. Since they weren't visibly labeled in any such manner this often became confusing for prospective parents or foster families as they screened potential candidates. Randy and his siblings were selected for adoption by both strangers and close relatives asking for permission and release from Betty. She, however, was determined to keep them together until Melinda was five years old, at which time all the children could go to school while she worked. Betty was also saving her paychecks to allow her to move her family into a small home that she and her former husband had purchased through the G.I. Bill. That time would have to wait.

Randy was only five years old now and Melinda not quite four. At this particular stage, Randy's group was led around the neighborhood for a daily walk. The elderly people, many sitting on their front porches, loved to see the children on their walks. One time as they were passing by, a widow curiously asked if the children knew any songs they could sing for her. Most of the children were pretty introverted, but Randy loved to sing and wasn't shy to raise his hand. So, he started singing as his peers stared, smiled, and giggled at him. The little lady, also smiling and laughing, was so pleased and impressed that she offered all the children cookies from a big plate she had standing by, just in case. This continued to happen throughout the weeks ahead. The little lady had shared this singing experience with her friends and Randy became the candy-cookie ticket for his companions throughout the neighborhood. As Christmas time approached, it seemed every home at which they stopped to sing, now with all of the children singing together in unison, had either cookies or candy as their reward. It was a joyful experience for the seniors, and even more so for the children.

Two weeks before the actual date of Christmas, the Home was visited by a charitable group wishing to donate gifts for all the children. They came with hot cocoa and cookies and helped decorate a large live donated spruce tree in the main TV meeting room. Most of the children had never seen, or even imagined, such a beautiful Christmas tree. Silvery tinsel, ornaments, bright colored lights, and the fascinating bubble lights adorned the tree. The staff circled strings of popcorn all over the tree; round and around to the large star on top.

4

PLASTIC SOLDIERS

The following week before Christmas, several of the children were selected to visit a local radio station. One by one they would go into the sound booth and sit down with the disc jockey. He would interview them and ask their ages, favorite animals, games, etc., and then inquire what they wanted most for Christmas. When it was Randy's turn he informed the DJ that he wanted an army set, the kind with little plastic soldiers and equipment; a popular gift shortly after World War II. Evidently one of the counselors in attendance had mentioned to the DJ that Randy loved to sing, and would sing to all the neighbors around the Home. This prompted the DJ to ask Randy what his favorite Christmas song was. Randy told him it was "I'm Dreaming of a White Christmas." So Randy was asked to sing the song on the air. Randy sang right through it, not missing a word or note. The small group left the radio station on their own happy note. Lots of hugs and candy canes sent them on their way. Finally, Christmas Day arrived. Every one of the kids in the Home was gathered in the large meeting room. The huge tree was lit up with the star at the top shining brightly. The counselors all stood around the mound of presents under the tree for eighty plus children. The Dean of the Home, wonderful, sweet and wise Mrs. Deitz, started passing out the gifts that had been donated by the charitable community, all marked with the children's first names. One by one, the children received their gifts, and then excitedly returned to their spots on the floor. Randy watched as Mrs. Deitz lifted a huge package and then called his name. He popped up and weaved his way through the crowd to pick up his gift. Randy's eyes seemed to get larger and larger as he walked toward the huge box. When he sat down, he excitedly ripped the bow and wrappings off of the package, wondering what was inside. His first glance at the unwrapped cardboard box revealed he had received exactly what he had wished. Hundreds of little green army men in every imaginable fighting position, scores of tiny motorcycles, jeeps, and transports were right in front of his eyes! Before long, all of the children were sitting in a pile of shredded wrapping paper enjoying their gifts. What a wonderful exciting Christmas it was. That army set would see a lot of action in the nearby miniature sandbox foxholes, trenches, and bunkers. It would remain, over many Christmases and years, Randy's most memorable Christmas gift, up to this time. The soldiers would see much more action when taken out to the sandbox! Christmas and the week-long holiday vacations went by all too fast at the Children's Home. Winter brought icy, freezing, snowy weather throughout the Midwest, especially in Wichita, Kansas, the very "heart" of America! While the dramatic weather was a beautiful sight, it created a harsh winter environment. Of course there were a few snowmen built and snowball fights to be had, but the extreme weather meant fewer trips and visits, and much more time confined inside the building. Storybook readings, games, chores, and meals now occupied most of the the children's days. When they were able to venture outside, it became a goal to spot red squirrels running through the snow and up into the trees. Eisenhower had won the election in a landslide, so most of the adults seemed to be in good spirits, but the children's focus was now on upcoming spring and summertime.

5

OKLA-HOME-AAAH

As the seasons continued to change spring had sprung, and the longer, warmer days improved everyone's mood and perspective. For Randy and his siblings, that meant more days outside catching frogs and crawdads in the nearby tiny meandering stream that ran under the trees and along the property border. Perhaps more visits with their mom would occur or maybe even a chance to visit Mema and Pepa for a weekend in Oklahoma City! In fact, Randy's grandparents had already planned a visit to Wichita late in the spring, and wanted to take Randy and Melinda back to their home in Oklahoma City for a little vacation. The drive to Oklahoma City took about three hours, which could have been daunting and tiring, considering they were cooped up and confined to the backseat of the aging blue Plymouth. But Randy hardly ever had a dull moment anywhere, except perhaps his long night in the dining room with the green stuff. While Pepa drove, Randy and Melinda would play the alphabet game as billboards and roadsigns passed by, identify every kind of animal that could be seen from the car, and look for any and every unusual or new visual discovery. Randy would never ask "are we there yet?" on any road trip, ever! He loved to travel! After playing games for a couple of hours, Randy leaned over the front seat and, out of the blue, blurted out to Mema and Pepa that, "I bet I know fifty songs I can sing!" Pepa, not knowing exactly what to expect, took him at his word, saying, "Okay, let's hear 'em." Randy was still singing over an hour later as they pulled into the driveway with Melinda sound asleep. Mema and Pepa simply looked at each other, shook their heads in amazement, and unloaded the car and kids.

It was a wonderful weekend in Oklahoma City. The little wood frame house had trees all around it, a big front porch, and was located twenty five feet from the railroad line in a very poor section of Oklahoma City. The trains coupled, stopped, and started right outside the little guest bedroom. The clashes of the cars coming together, and the screeching, clanking metal noises throughout the night made it virtually impossible to get a good night's sleep for Randy and Melinda. There was a candy store right across the street from the house with a very generous owner who loved children! A church Buffalo Head Nickel could go a very long way there! And when the grandfolks would take the kids out for a walk across nearby Main Street, there were street vendors selling all kinds of food from temporary wooden stalls and tables, set up and down the sidewalks, like a current day farmers market. Pepa was a finish carpenter by trade, and had a little shop in his wooden, detached, single car garage. He had made some changes to their little home over the years, including an extended screened-in summer porch bedroom, and a pop-out breakfast nook surrounded by windows next to the kitchen. This was a favorite meeting spot since the family would gather there for most of its meals, especially Pepa's popular "Frittos & Dr Pepper" lunch cuisine. Pepa would fan out the Frittos, as he called them, on his handmade wooden table before the sandwiches were served in an effort to make the meal look even more inviting and extravagant. Pepa's sense of humor, wisdom, and gentle, loving nature made him a favorite with everyone who knew him.

Pepa, Harry, was a real man in every sense; deeply spiritual, physically strong, compassionate, affectionate, loving, romantic, persevering, engaging, and with a joyful sense of humor. He had found his way through the Great Depression, served in the Navy in WWI on a battleship as a Naval nurse, raised four children, and possessed a tremendous work ethic; all of this with only a grade school education. It seemed there was nothing he couldn't do. He knew when to shake hands, embrace in a hug, or give a kiss, and never struggled to hold back tears that were meant to flow. He and his wife, Margie, realized very early on in their sixty three year marriage that there was no such thing as a "division of labor." Each person did what they could do, whenever and whatever needed to be done. Mema and Pepa were strong role models and examples to their children, grandchildren and countless others. One of Randy's favorite stories about his grandfather was the time his carpenter tools were stolen out of the trunk of his rickety car. Someone had ripped off the latch and taken all of his tools. After surveying his loss and realizing that his means of income would be severely tested during the current deep depression, he simply said "Well, whoever took these things must have needed them more than I do." Even so, Pepa would meagerly feed the homeless and vagabonds at his back porch almost daily during those years, as well as caring for his wife and four children. Margie, Mema, was his equal in integrity, love, generosity, and character. They seemed the perfect couple in every phase and stage of matrimony. They provided a perfect example of two people becoming one.

6

ALMOST THERE!

The years at the Children's Home continued to unfold; most notably marked by Mickey's attempt to flee the premises with two friends, and hoping to jump a freight car on the nearby railroad in the middle of the night! The three of them were quickly discovered by a family that stopped them and asked them why they were out so late. Mickey said they were Boy Scouts trying to qualify for a couple more badges. The police were notified, and the three "scouts" were returned to the Home without their badges! And, finally, Melinda would be turning five soon and could be enrolled in grade school the coming fall; a goal Betty had originally set when she first considered the Children's Home. Randy was now almost seven, Mickey nine, and Melody eleven. Betty would have to notify the renters of her little G.I. home that they would have to vacate by the beginning of summer. She had earned and saved enough to make the monthly house payment. But, an overwhelming transition was about to take place for the young single mother.

Betty's friends from church and her three workplaces

joined together to help with the move and prepare for the "home-going." Used and donated furniture, appliances, dishes and utensils, utility contracts, upcoming school enrollments, etc. all had to be arranged. It was daunting, tedious, time-consuming, and relatively expensive, considering her limited income. But, it all slowly came together, and the next step was to round up her children and lead them to a new life in their own home; a first-time experience.

7

AT LAST!

None of the children seemed able to recall the exact date or time of their departure from the Children's Home. Perhaps it was too unbelievable or exciting. In any case, that part of their early history was just that...History! Upon arriving and entering the 30' x 30' "mansion," they were overjoyed! The simple squarish white tract house on a corner lot had two bedrooms the size of two bathrooms, with one bathroom the size of a bathtub, for two girls, two boys, and a single mom. A miniature kitchen and dining area seemed quite adequate since it was now their own. The living room could just barely accommodate a 9' x 12' rollout carpet. There was a gas log fireplace that no one could remember ever seeing a burning fire of any kind, wood or gas, in it. The only fires in the house were set by Mickey, who started several small fires throughout the house and basement over the years. A tiny concrete porch welcomed visitors, and an attached three quarter car garage was available should a car ever be acquired. Fortunately, with Kansas being in the "tornado bowl" there was an unfinished basement, that would very soon become both a tornado shelter and the boys' Man Cave; one in the same. Until those options were needed, the basement served as a play room/game room for the kids, and an operating space for an old styled wringer washer placed over the basement water drain. After washing and wringing, clothes were hung on outside clothes lines to dry. The heating system for the house was a gas furnace that emitted heat through the wood floor, opened up by a 3' x 4' single metal grate in the dining room; a popular spot for the children to hover during the winter months. Snow would melt off their pants and boots, making hissing sounds as it hit the furnace. Their bodies were warmed and the family dog, Ace, adopted out of a cardboard box as a puppy, would start to thaw out and lose the hairy icicles covering his heavy black and white coat. Ace loved the snow, but always came out of it looking like a scary wolf from a Hemingway novel.

Finally, the transition was complete. The children loved the neighborhood, and quickly made many friends up and down the adjoining streets. There was a public golf course across busy Hillside Street that led to downtown Wichita. Randy would occasionally caddy there (his very first job!). He would find errant golf balls in his adjacent backyard almost daily, and then sell them back to golfers the next day...his introduction to capitalism. He would also shovel snow, mow lawns with a manual reel mower ($.50), and join Melinda in selling used comic books at the edge of the busy street. The shopping center across Bluff Street had an IGA grocery store, home of Mickey's first real job, a drugstore, barbershop, and a hamburger diner, all employed by staff that loved the four kids. The IGA store was the scene of Randy's one and only theft of two empty milk jugs at the corner pick-up location. There was also a large vacant field in back of the center where the neighborhood kids would gather to dig foxholes, play football and baseball, or have clay clod fights while using trash can lids as shields. Only a few minor injuries were sustained over the years. Safety and security were provided by every parent and merchant in the tight knit community. It was the perfect home and neighborhood for this family.

8

LIFE AT 1402 N. BLUFF

As they settled in, it seemed as if everything got better and better each day, week, and month. Randy and Mickey established the basement as their "Territory" with bunkbeds, an old couch, a small throw rug, one lamp, and a chest of drawers. However, the hot water heater was also in the basement. It quit working one day, so Randy decided he would re-ignite it. Well, there was gas in the air, and then an explosion in Randy's eyes as he struck the match. No more eyebrows and a few raspy skin sores. Nothing more.

A Monopoly set would remain in place on the cement floor for continued weekly real estate transactions. The boys would evolve the board game to where they would play without using the paper money; simply writing down the cash exchanges. They would often extend leniency to each other to prolong the game.

Randy somehow managed to acquire two small white rat roommates, Ratzo and Ritzo. They were kept in a compact wire cage in the basement. One day, they were "found missing," an oxymoron that caused Betty to become unhinged!

This event far exceeded an earlier experience she had of finding Randy's newfound skink lizard on her bed pillow one night. Randy had placed the shiny, beautiful, blue/green, three inch skink in the screened window at the head of Betty's bed. Unfortunately, she opened her window that night. Fortunately, Betty did not faint, and Lizzy was quickly rounded up, immediately granted a commuted sentence, and released. Alas, the rats were found in the basement days later; one missing, and the other alive and well, and quickly given away by Executive Order, aka Betty, at the first opportunity! A small rat burial ceremony was held in the backyard for Ratzo, dead or alive, may he RIP. Only two people were in attendance.

There would be other more suitable, appropriate, and "approved" pets along the way. First of all, a stray mama cat, taken in a few months earlier, decided to have kittens one night as the children were spread out on the living room floor watching a twelve inch black and white box television. She came over to Randy, crawled up on his back as he laid face down on the floor, and dug her claws into his back skin through his t-shirt. She then proceeded to have three little pink babies. Melody placed them, one at a time, in a cardboard box with a towel in it. They were named Snap, Crackle, and Pop, the Rice Krispie Kitties. The children quit watching television and spent the whole evening staring while visually inspecting the wriggling little triplets. All the while Melody attempted to share her limited birds and the bees "wisdom." The adorable little kittens found homes around the neighborhood in a very short time, but it seemed a loss to the kids.

Sometime after that, another small homeless creature showed up in the yard; this time, a yellowish "Disney dog." He was small, active, playful, and seemed to love the kids.

He had no tags and no one was aware of an owner or from where he may have come. So, he was there, and "possession being nine tenths of the law," he was theirs! The little guy was dubbed "Fritzy" and remained in the family for several years, then simply slipped away one day as quickly as he had come.

A friend had given Betty a used light green Henry J car that the children nicknamed "the grasshopper." Betty had also been offered a new job selling radio time with a local radio station, where they soon discovered she also had a gift for writing commercials. Now there would be just one job instead of the two or three she was juggling while trying to manage her new household through Melody and numerous check in phone calls. Just prior to accepting her new radio career Betty had started to date an officer she had met at the local Air Force Base; Hank, whom she dated for several years.

In the meantime, Randy was nabbed by two railroad detectives while he and a friend were found digging foxholes along the railroad tracks. Illegal. Because of his age they declined to charge him as he stood before Betty; accused, and obviously guilty, as the dirt on his hands and jeans would attest. Another event during the transition included Randy and his siblings talking Betty into adopting the previously mentioned Ace, a small, at the time, baby Border Collie - German Shepherd mix puppy. He was brought to their front door in a cardboard box by two young kids. Ace was the last of the litter. The children coaxed Hank into supporting their request, claiming "he won't get too big." Hank, however, having studied the huge paws on the little black and white puppy, knew better. But he still endorsed their plan! And indeed, Ace would blossom into a beautiful, large ninety pound friend and guardian for his new family. Ace would remain the "top-dog" for fifteen years. He became "the standard" for every dog that would follow.

There would be many more personal events that Randy would recall in the few remaining years at their new home. The freedom of simply roaming the neighborhood, snowy winters for sledding on the golf course slopes into the iced over creek beds, snowball fights, Christmas tree forts, and building huge snowmen were wonderful.

On one particularly cold icy evening, Randy had drifted across the street over to the drugstore. The heavy snow covered Oliver Street was highlighted by the bright street lights. He ordered up his favorite drink, a ten cent Cherry Coke, at the counter, and sat there by himself listening to the jukebox until a young man came flying in the door from the parking lot. Freezing wind blew snow flurries behind him. He leaned against the door to push it closed and then sat on the stool next to Randy. He excitedly started explaining to Mr. Fowler, the store owner, that he had just lost his wedding ring while adjusting his tire chains due to the increasingly hazardous storm. He said if by any chance the ring was found and turned in there, he would gladly pay a reward. Randy, overhearing the conversation, and upon hearing the word "reward," sprinted out the door in the direction of where the loss had occurred. Miraculously, he found the ring in the snow after about five minutes. He came running back in the door shouting "I found it. I found it." No one could believe it until Randy held the shiny gold band out in his palm. The young man was astounded and very thankful. He reached into his pocket to pull out some reward money. At that same moment, Melody came in the front door, worried about Randy's absence now after about fifteen minutes. She immediately asked Randy what was going on when she saw the money in his hand. The young man explained to her what had happened, smiling all the way. Melody, a hopeless romantic, told Randy there was no way he was going to keep the reward money for finding the man's wedding ring. She demanded that Randy return the money. All Randy could say was "but, but..." as he reluctantly returned the folded bills. The man insisted that Randy keep the reward, but Melody insisted, all the more, that he would not. She walked Randy straight home. The experience was now simply, and rightly, a good deed. And, a very good lesson. One of many that Melody would share over the years to come.

9

ANOTHER CHANGE ON THE WAY

Afer about four or five years of settling in, the garage had been turned into Randy and Mickey's bedroom, thanks to Pepa's carpentry skills. During most of that time, Betty had been seeing Hank, and the relationship was growing. Frequent visits by Hank included trips to the movies and the local burger joint, watching TV together, and Hank carrying the smaller children to bed late at night. Three of the children thoroughly admired and adored Hank; but Melody, being a young teenage girl, had some reservations. Randy would ask Betty, almost daily, if she and Hank were going to get married. She never gave a direct answer, but hopeful all the same. Finally, Hank announced he was going to be transferred to the Pentagon in Washington, D.C. Betty wept as he departed, and the children shared her disappointment, figuring that was the end of that episode. However, and this is a big however, Hank called Betty from D.C. and proposed marriage to her. He planned to fly back, get married in California and take Betty on a honeymoon in Carmel. After that, they could do what needed to be done at the house, and then drive the family from Kansas to Virginia. Heads were spinning, kids jumping, and hearts pumping. Another unbelievable change was about to happen in the lives held together through faith, Betty's perseverance, and the Wichita Children's Home. On top of all that, Hank actually wanted to legally adopt the four children as his own! He asked the children for their permission. Melody was the only one slightly reluctant; the other three were all in. A father, taking them in as his own, a name change, becoming heirs, moving across the nation; a story of Biblical impact. It was almost too much to imagine, but the plan was in motion.

Mema and Pepa drove to the house from Oklahoma City, and proceeded to help clean and clear out the household items. Many things were simply tossed out and the home furnishings were set outside to sell. Hardly anything actually sold, and Betty ended up paying to have the furniture hauled away. It was humiliating, but necessary. In the meantime, Hank had traded his very cool white Buick sedan for a flamingo colored Oldsmobile station wagon; which said a lot about his impending identity/role change. The wagon was filled with personal belongings, four kids, and two adults. And late in the process of packing up, the side back window was rolled down, and Ace, making sure he wasn't forgotten, jumped up and in through the window and landed on top of the baggage like he was a greyhound! As the newlyweds joined in; everybody was set to go! No rats, lizards, or cats on this trip... just Ace and one happy family!

10

LIVING THE LIFE

I t was now the middle of August and the journey back to the East Coast seemed like an awesome summer vacation for everyone. There were hotel stops with swimming pools, dining out daily along the way, sightseeing, and lots of games and singing. The children were seeing sights they had never imagined. Their first place of residency was in Hank's "luxury" D.C. apartment. The new family received many stares as they traversed through the lobby. When they finally moved from the apartment, they pulled up in the driveway of the home that Hank and Betty had rented. The children were totally overwhelmed! A two story large brick house with trees all over the expansive grassy lot in a quiet, private, upscale neighborhood. The children, again, quickly made friends; Melody and the boy next door, Mickey and the girl down the street, while Randy and Melinda simply enjoyed a neighborhood to explore. Ace also made a friend next door; an elderly middle sized dog named Foxy, a friend he would eventually save from a vicious attack by a bulldog that had escaped its household. With a number of adjoining neighbors standing by, Ace ripped the bulldog off of Foxy and sent him running home. The new neighbors felt forever indebted.

There were many more transitional events for the kids. Michael, aka Mickey, had started singing in the eighth grade, and was amazing people with his voice by the time he was thirteen! HMS Pinafore was his first big role at school, and the reviews were overwhelming. He would continue on with his talent through high school musicals, encores, and extended nightly performances, and ultimately, a full university tuition music scholarship at Kansas State University, the USAF Singing Sergeants, and a European opera career for nearly twenty one years! Melody was a leader in everything that she did. She was an excellent dancer, academically astute, and extremely compassionate toward every stray animal and every "gone wrong" rebel boyfriend she would meet. She became a juvenile probation officer before her passing. Randy and Melinda would remain in the shadows of their older siblings for quite a while. Michael would serve as Randy's disciplinarian for church attendance and chores, while Melody would try to nurture Melinda through difficult times. But beyond that, a larger event was about to unfold.

The school year was approaching and things had settled down after the move. Betty's new career was about to take off as she had been chosen by U.S. Senator Frank Carlson from Kansas to be his press secretary. She had been recommended for the position by the man she worked for at the radio station in Kansas. Betty had won the award for top radio sales two years in a row. She became the first woman to earn that award, which was an accomplishment that helped move her career upward. She just kept moving ahead.

Every day now, Hank and Betty drove together into

Washington, D.C. to the Pentagon and the Senate office building for their jobs. The boys would occasionally visit them at their places of work. Randy and Michael even got to play basketball in the Pentagon's gym with General Curtis LeMay and many other military officers. General LeMay was unknown to them until after a very rough game when a captain asked Randy, "Do you know who you were guarding?" Randy and Michael would often encounter many politicians in the Senate building.

A troubling thing for Randy upon first arriving in Virginia was noticing the restroom signs and drinking fountains that posted "colored," or "whites only." He had no idea what any of this was about. Relationships with black friends in Kansas were rare, but always comfortable. Randy would fondly remember the time in Wichita when his mom was approached by the black man who picked up the two large cans of burned trash ashes in the backyard each week. One day she and the kids were hanging clothes on the clothesline when the man came across the back lawn and informed her that one of his truck tires had gone flat. It would take fifteen dollars to replace it, and could she possibly help him out? Money was still very tight at this stage, but she walked straight into the house and brought out fifteen dollars from her coffee can emergency savings. The man was so grateful that he picked up the trash ashes for Betty free of charge for three months. There was always something new and different to learn. The restroom signs would be just the beginning of experiencing the many differences, changes, challenges, and opportunities to which this newly relocated family would have to adjust. It would be a "whirlwind."

They would very soon have "racial interaction" in their new Virginia home. There was a small black community of very low income families on the other side of the backyard wall fence. Randy and his siblings would often pass by some of the younger residents on their way to school. Their first Halloween in the new home had trick-or-treaters from all over the neighborhood, including the very poor black community beyond the stone wall. Randy remembers two young cute black children coming to the door; about five and seven years old. They rang the door bell, and shouted "trick-or-treat!" Randy held out the big bowl of candy for them. Each child took just one small piece, saying "thank you," and started to turn away. Randy said, "Wait! Come back and take some more." The younger little boy lit up and, oh boy, started raking candy from the bowl into his bag. His older sister could only say "Me o' my! Look at dat candy go!" Randy thought it was hilarious, fun, and heartwarming. There would be many more new home episodes in the years to come.

Marriage for a forty one year old confirmed bachelor military officer, to a now thirty six year old divorcee with four children; two teens and two near teens, seemed unlikely, crazy, and potentially hazardous! Hank would later say he only wanted to do this once. This marriage adoption challenge for a West Point military pilot who had flown sixty six missions in Europe during World War II, was quite possibly Hank's bravest endeavor ever, as we constantly reminded him years later! Two years after their marriage Betty and Hank would have a baby boy, little John, another brave endeavor! What an exciting addition for the entire family! John had older parents, but, eventually four teenage siblings to keep him busy. Ace would walk circles around John to ensure his protection, and ward off any kind of threat; human or beast, wherever he might be.

11

YOUNG ADULTHOOD

There would be two more household moves, new friends to make, high school events, sports, music, and eventually off to college for the four budding adults. Melody was the scholar, Michael the singer, Randy the athletic, social romantic artist, and Melinda undecided, as of yet, but with many talents. Melody would be the first to marry, after sorting through her many candidates. Michael would receive his draft notice while he and Randy were working in Los Angeles making deliveries to Hollywood movie sets. Michael would soon find out, from a college friend, that there was an immediate opening in the USAF Singing Sergeants in Washington, D.C. By this time, Betty and Hank had moved from D.C. to Anchorage, Alaska to help Hank's mom and dad after the huge Alaska earthquake had nearly destroyed the small coastal city of Seward in March of 1964. So, Michael and Randy would have to drive to Washington, D.C. for the Singing Sergeants audition. This was no small task since the opening was only good for three days from the time of his friend's phone call. Michael and Randy packed whatever they could in Michael's little red Volkswagen beetle with socks and underwear packed around the car battery underneath the backseat. Everything else, including Michael's guitar, filled the rest of the limited space. They headed out at dusk that evening, sometime in August of '65. As they left, they looked back from the freeway to see large fires in Los Angeles! It would be days later until they would discover that there had been riots in the city of Watts that night. The drive to Washington, D.C. from Los Angeles was long and arduous. It was a continuous fifty four hour trip. They would remember listening to the radio at midnight the night they departed, and the announcer stated, "It's twelve o'clock midnight, and one hundred degrees in Needles, California!" A short stop in Oklahoma City to see Pepa and Mema, and they were on their way again. The desperate trip was hot, dusty, and sweaty. Their white t-shirts and wheat jeans were dark brown by the time they arrived at the very last hour, for Michael's audition. He was called forward and asked his vocal range. Michael, in turn, asked what they needed. His range allowed him to sing whatever they wanted. He qualified and was accepted for the position, and would soon be enlisted in the United States Air Force Singing Sergeants, traveling around the world for four years. Tough!

Melinda would eventually get married a few years after college, and have two beautiful boys. Her military family would relocate often, moving from base to base every few years. Michael would finish his four year commitment in the Singing Sergeants and attend the Music Academy of the West in Montecito, California through the generosity of a sweet wealthy patron. After that he was offered a contract to sing opera in Germany, a career lasting twenty one years. He would eventually become the father of two beautiful sons. Randy would travel to Anchorage, Alaska each summer to visit his family and work for the Alaska railroad freight line and rail section gang. In his third year of college he would meet the love of his life one night at a party, the day after breaking up with a former girlfriend. He announced to his doubtful heckling roommates that night that he had met the woman he would marry! One week after meeting Sheryl, Randy left for his third summer in Alaska. He was offered a job as a radio announcer for the number one station in Anchorage; a job he thoroughly enjoyed. He played all of the top forty hits and had all the latest national teletype news! The first night that he was asked to do the television news, Robert Kennedy was shot in Los Angeles. With only two minutes of local news to present and nothing for national news on the teletype; "Moose stops traffic in downtown Anchorage," and "Three arrested in bar room brawl on Fourth Avenue," would have to do. The teletype stopped all national and international news releases just prior to his airtime. Randy felt like he had died a thousand times! Maybe his boss was right when he said "You have a perfect face for radio!" Betty and Hank felt his pain. However, over the course of his radio and TV time, and volunteer life guard at Goose Lake, he would write to Sheryl daily, as she would to him; eventually proposing marriage to her. While visiting Melody in San Francisco they got engaged. Melody immediately asked Sheryl if she was sure she wanted to marry Randy; Sheryl re-affirmed, and then returned to Denver to resume teaching kindergarten. Randy flew back to Kansas State University for another shot at a degree in law. He would, however, have an opportunity to join the Kansas Air National Guard during the Vietnam War era, thereby avoiding the confusion of that war. But, he would soon have to leave for basic training. With one week of notice, he and Sheryl planned their wedding one day before

Easter in 1969. After a very "exotic" honeymoon in Oklahoma City, Randy was off to Lackland Air Force Base in San Antonio, Texas just five days after their marriage. About this time Melody was diagnosed with colon cancer at the age of twenty seven. She was soon hospitalized, spurring Randy and Sheryl to move to California from Kansas after just one year living in Betty's house in Wichita. Hank and Betty had already retired in California. After almost three years of marriage, and a week before Randy's twenty fifth birthday, Melody would pass away; a loss that would affect the family in many ways for years to come. Providentially, Sheryl shared the exact same birth date with Melody, thereby creating an annual reminder of Melody and her life.

12

MOVING ON

Randy was grateful for the short time he had with Melody, and he and Sheryl were happy with their move to California. Randy was very much the entrepreneur and started two businesses on his own; a fleet washing business and three frozen yogurt shops. He loved to work, and never had a job that he didn't like. His many jobs included being a caddy, odd jobs, comic books sales, paint store salesman, McDonald's, KuKu's Burgers, senior living assistant, fraternity busboy, Hollywood movie sets, San Ysidro Ranch restaurant floor manager, UCSB cafeteria manager, and Goleta Valley Community Center Executive Director. Sheryl taught school for ten years and helped start the frozen yogurt business in three locations. The frozen yogurt idea was about five years ahead of its time and eventually faltered. That failure forced the sale of the home they had built. They used a large part of their equity to pay off business debts, and moved to Solvang. Randy was dejected and unemployed. Fortunately, Sheryl had secured an excellent job with Santa Barbara Research Center (which later became Raytheon) at pretty much an entry level position and quickly climbed each step of the Corporate ladder and retired twenty eight years later. During the meager times Randy was able to sell parts of his baseball card collection that he had saved from his early childhood; 1958 - 1962, plus later additions. If they were a little short for groceries or gasoline...so long '58 Mickey Mantle!

Marriage was a little difficult the first seven years, primarily because of Randy's creative temperament, background, and personality. An experimental last chance desperation one year trip was definitely called for. Randy and Sheryl sold their home and bought a small class C motorhome and traveled ten months and twenty four thousand miles around the United States through Canada, Alaska, Florida, and the East Coast with Bishop, a large German Shepherd, and Foxy Lady, a diminutive Pomeranian. This adventure would prove to be very beneficial in getting past some rough spots. Within a year of moving from Goleta, California to Solvang, California they would join a church and be baptized together by Dr. Jack MacArthur. Their lives and marriage would continue to grow and heal as they were challenged and emptied through various circumstances. Unable to have children, they did many things together; just the two of them. This was great for Randy, but exhausting for Sheryl. They would become very invested in church life. Sheryl led the choir for eight years. Randy started singing and leading Bible studies, social events, retreats, mission trips, youth groups, and youth sports.

Life would move on; illnesses and family losses, including many friends. Brother John would marry a beautiful young lady with a son from a previous marriage, and they would then bear a sweet little baby girl. The first girl, granddaughter and niece in the family! Sadly she passed away at the age of twenty two. Many Christmases, anniversaries, and birthdays would be celebrated over the years. Life was moving forward. Randy's dreams of playing centerfield for the Yankees, being a disc jockey, romantic crooner, or successful businessman were replaced by a much better plan.

Sixty five years after Randy's Christmas gift of plastic soldiers at the Children's Home, his most memorable Christmas gift would now forever be a large wooden cross standing over the valley, lit up at night. It was given to Randy and Sheryl by a hard working young man who had helped them with home projects over the years. Mario, and his new beautiful bride, Katie, delivered the 12' X 8' hand made cross; beveled, varnished, sturdy, and magnificent, on Christmas day! Mario set it in concrete, attached the crossbar, and strung the solar lights around the cross's perimeter! Positive comments would come from every part of the Santa Ynez Valley! It was a fitting reminder for Randy, now seventy, of how far he had come from plastic soldiers at the Wichita Children's Home to a wooden cross on the hill in Solvang. He would forever be reminded that God always had a plan for his life, a far better plan than we have for ourselves. From birth to the Children's Home, to a new dad, and then Jesus in my life. A very providential journey by God's design! Be prepared! Every day may provide a new beginning, not of your own doing!

∽

Made in the USA
Middletown, DE
28 March 2023

27055462R00027